My Little Book of Big Questions

Britta Teckentrup

My Little Book of
Big Questions

Prestel

Munich · London · New York

How will I see the world
when I am **grown** up?

Will I find my **place** in life?

Why do I feel that you're close by?

What will **become** of me?

Will I be a famous
football player?

Will I be able to **fly** someday?

Is the world **inside** or **outside** of me?

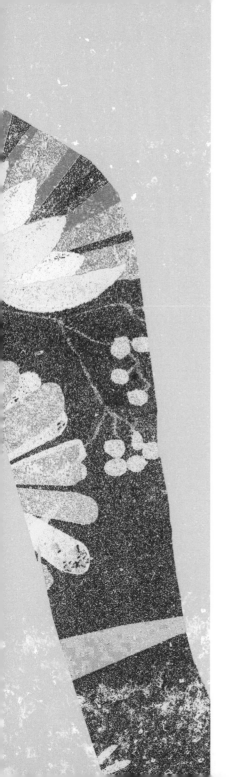

Do **flowers**, when they grow,
feel the same as I do when I grow?

Why do we always
have to **argue?**

Why are they so **mean** to me?

Will we **get along** again?

Why do we all want
to be **popular?**

Why do you **understand** me
so much better than anybody else?

Will you be my friend?

How come that even though the sun
is so far away, we can still feel its warmth?

Why am I **afraid**
of what I don't know**?**

Why is **nature** so colourful?
Is it just for me?
Or for all people?
What about the animals?

What if the **winter** never ends?

Will he **like** me?

Will he **kiss** me?

Can I reach for the **stars?**

When somebody is very old and dies,
and a **tree** grows out of his grave,
is he then the tree?

Do **birds** like to fly?

How do birds **see** the world?

If I could **fly**, would the birds
think I am one of them?

Why can't I fly?
What is it that pulls me
to the **ground?**

When an **eagle** gathers food for its offspring,
is that similar to a human being going to work?

Why do I like a person who is completely **different** from myself ...

... and has completely different things in his head?

Is it possible to understand
the whole universe?

Am I special?

Is it good to step out of line?

Why do most people mostly do the same ...

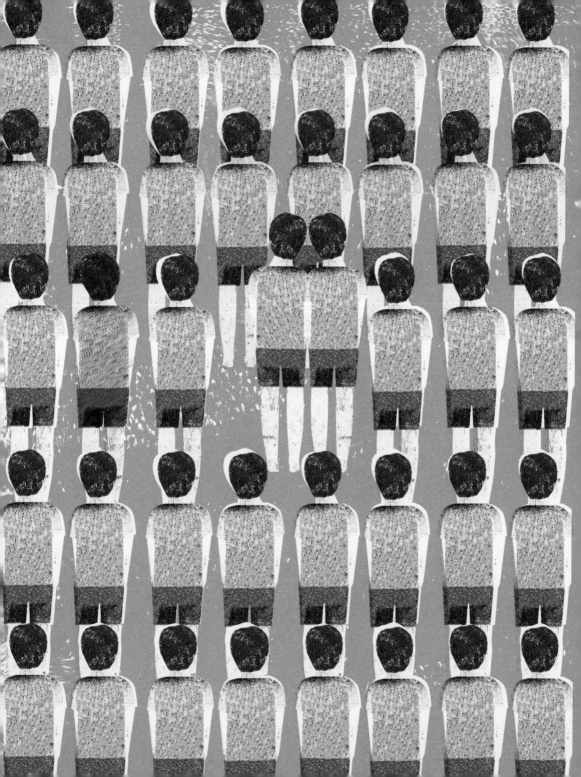

... whereas some
do not?

If we **build** upon each other, is it harder
for the one who goes first and easier
for the ones who follow?

Why do I always come across **walls?**

Or are the walls simply in my head?

What **secrets** are
others hiding from me ...

... and what are they up to?

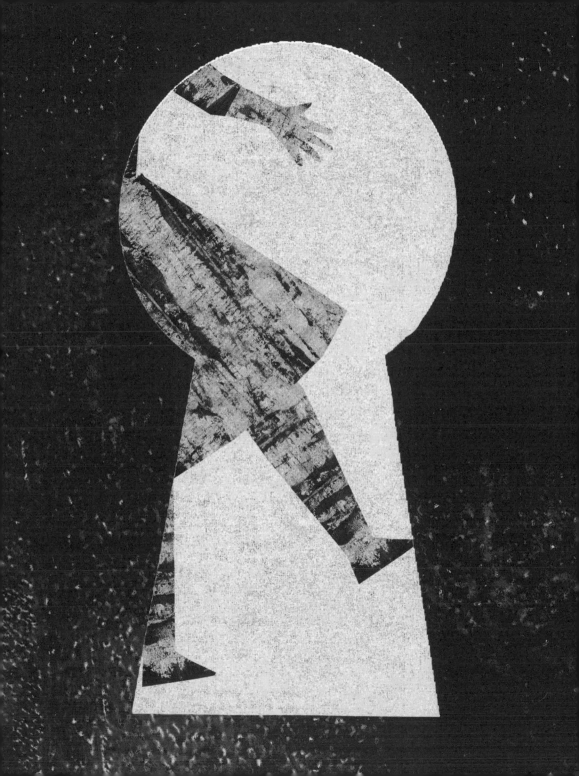

Do they hold the key to
things I don't understand?

Why do more and more secrets come to light after one has been revealed?

Why do things seem to happen all by themselves when we dance?

Does that turn us into
different **creatures?**

Will we be **enchanted** …

... and carried off into
another world?

Why can't everything stay the way it is?

Why do people have the least
to do with one another the more
they are **pushed together?**

Why do some people
turn **nasty** when
they are in
a large group?

When we **dream** about two people
that seem more or less similar,
are they one person in real life?

Do **twins** want to stay together forever?

Will they still
be **together** when
they're old?

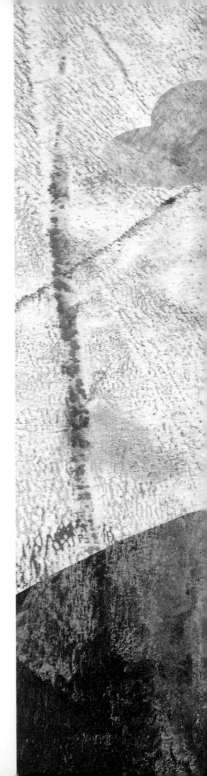

Do they always follow
the same paths in life?

When one twin has died,
will the other **follow** soon?

Can you **hold** me?
Forever**?**

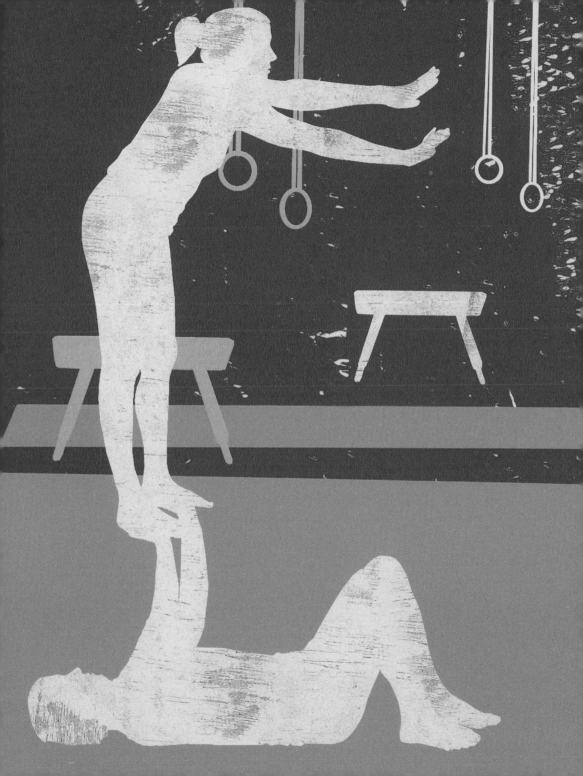

Where are you?

Will I **find** what I'm looking for?

Do you feel **light-headed**
every now and then?

When you can't come up with
any ideas, does it feel like all of the
doors in your head are closed?

And when they suddenly **open**,
do you have thousands of ideas?

Why can't it always be **spring?**

If I make myself really small, I might fit through that door!

I wonder what is **hidden** behind it?

Why do we say that you fall into a deep sleep when you actually fall into **dreamland?**

Are dreams as **true** as reality?

Is it possible to **share**
the same dream?

Why does everything feel so **real** in our dreams?

Does happiness mean that, you think of
nothing but **beautiful** things?

Why do I feel so good
when we are all together?

What exactly is the future?

What is the past?
Is it back then, when
these two were still young?
Or is it longer ago?
Or very much longer ago?
Or even before anything else?

Am I in **love?**

If I think long and hard,

will I discover the **meaning** of life?

Why am I feeling so small
when I am being **told off?**

Why are my thoughts going around in **circles?**

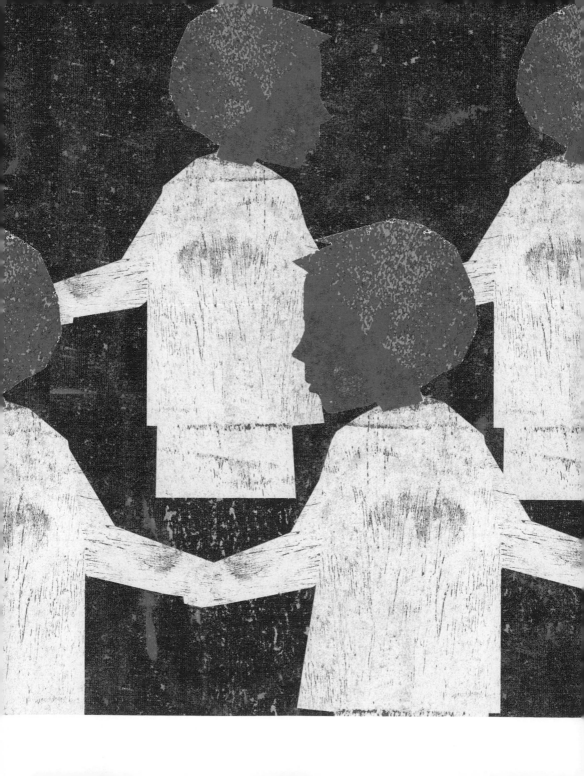

Why can I sort out my thoughts
much better when I **talk** about
them with somebody I like?

Will I be as wise as my grandmother?

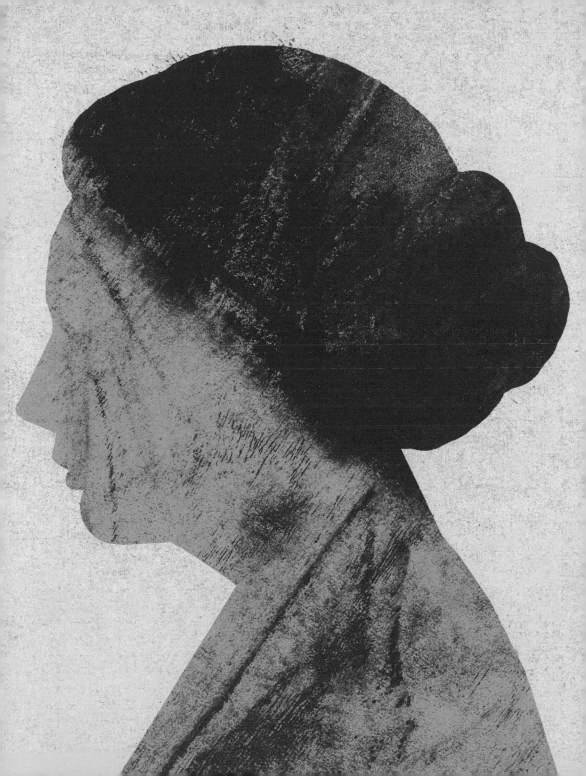

Do **animals** think?

Why are we afraid of jumping
when we feel so **brave** afterwards?

Why do we say
'jump in at the deep end'
when we decide to do something and
are not certain of the outcome?

Is it possible to think of nothing?

Why am I sometimes not **bored** at all when nothing happens?

Isn't it great to really feel alive?

Is it possible to feel too **happy?**

Why does the world seem
so much **bigger** when you
stand by the **sea?**

Why are some days
just **perfect** ...

Do you feel like **hugging**
the whole world every now and then ...

.... and just want to jump
and do **cartwheels?**

And do you sometimes have
a **longing** for something
but don't know exactly what it is?

Do you aim **high?**

Isn't it **fantastic**
just to enjoy dreaming**?**

Wouldn't it be great to walk
a **tightrope** without
the fear of falling down?

Don't we all aim high?

Do all people ask the same **questions?**

Prestel Publishing Ltd.
14-17 Wells Street
London W1T 3PD

Prestel Publishing
900 Broadway, Suite 603
New York, NY 10003

Library of Congress Control Number: 2018949224
A CIP catalogue record for this book is available from the British Library.

Copyediting: Brad Finger
Project management: Melanie Schöni
Production management: Susanne Hermann
Typesetting: textum GmbH, Feldafing
Printing and binding: DZS Grafik d.o.o.
Paper: Tauro

MIX
Papier aus verantwor-
tungsvollen Quellen
FSC® C106600

Verlagsgruppe Random House FSC® N001967

Printed in Slovenia

ISBN 978-3-7913-7376-8

www.prestel.com